Bea's Random Buzzings:
Sweet and Thorny

Bea's Random Buzzings: Sweet and Thorny

A Poetry Collection

Beatrice Diamond

iUniverse, Inc.
New York Lincoln Shanghai

Bea's Random Buzzings: Sweet and Thorny
A Poetry Collection

iUniverse books may be ordered through booksellers or by contacting:

iUniverse
2021 Pine Lake Road, Suite 100
Lincoln, NE 68512
www.iuniverse.com
1-800-Authors (1-800-288-4677)

Because of the dynamic nature of the Internet, any Web addresses or links contained in this book may have changed since publication and may no longer be valid.

The views expressed in this work are solely those of the author and do not necessarily reflect the views of the publisher, and the publisher hereby disclaims any responsibility for them.

Art and photographs by author with the exception of the two photographs accompanying "The Sad Tour." Those are by Sol Rubin.

ISBN: 978-0-595-42656-0 (pbk)
ISBN: 978-0-595-86984-8 (ebk)

Printed in the United States of America

The author acknowledges, with loving gratitude,
the editorial assistance of her daughter
Alyne Diamond Keneally

Contents

Preface . . . . *xi*

EMOTIONS

Writelock 3

Gift 5

Woman as Venus 7

Her Majesty 8

Woman and Man 9

A Baby's Cry 10

Duo 12

Progeny 13

Tear 14

Sequence 16

Wondrous Death 18

Hell Waiting 19

Joyous Paint 20

Versatile Dancing 21

Woeful Adolescence 23

Empty 25

Helpless 27

Sad Hide and Seek 29

Limiting Horizons 31

A New Day 32

Theater *33*

Time with You *35*

Ageless Elvis *36*

Her Adam *38*

SOCIAL ISSUES

Differences *41*

The Terror *43*

September 11, 2001: Two Minutes Left *44*

Contemplation on Tsunami *45*

The "New" New Orleans *47*

The Neophyte *48*

Challenge to Closure *49*

Korean Memorial *53*

The Sad Tour *54*

Gravestones *59*

Lower East Side Tenement Museum *60*

Boys Must Be Boys *62*

Shuttle Columbia *63*

Brainless Omnipotent Bells *64*

I Chose, I Fear, I Must *65*

Candidates' Debate *66*

The Public and the Not-So-Merry Political Scene *67*

NATURE: FLORA & FAUNA

The Gates *71*

Quick Succession *72*

Autumn Leaves *75*

Nature's Mood Music *76*

Snow's Cascade 77

Untitled 78

Untitled 78

A Deciduous Winter Tree's Love Ode to the Sun 79

Spring 80

Renewal: Tree And Woman 83

Dandelion 85

"Moonlight" 87

Carousel 89

Who's Birdbrained? 92

About the Author 95

Preface

What is more universal than a potpourri poetry menu
correlated to human emotions, life's beginnings and
endings, the beauty and ugliness of nature's power, and
man's inhumanity to man?

Bees search sweet targets in circuitous perpetual motion, buzzing among
available flora.

In *Bea's Buzzings: Sweet And Thorny*, I searched temperate, sensuous,
and disturbing targets, buzzing among this vast array of human issues,
favoring some for ruminating and annotating in poetic declaration. My
choice areas are the senses, social issues, and nature.

The selection of "sweet" issues includes emotions of love, joy, progeny,
hope, and caring; nature's beauty and bounty; and multiculturalism and
brotherhood.

"Thorny" human issues encompass death, the afterlife, war, nature's
wrath, genocide, disappointment, illness, and heavenly censure.

I respectfully submit my opinion on "social" issues and make no claim
to erudite thinking, expressing my thoughts to whomever reads and listens
to them.

Emotions

Writelock

I entered into the union
    with naiveté.
I did not heed the question,
     "Does anyone know just cause
     to show why these two should
     not be joined together?"
We were joined in writelock,
     Poetry and Novice Poet.

Only now do I hear
    just cause protests.
My own voice quietly whispers,
     "You've work projects waiting.
     There are chores to do."

I muffle the protests,
     happily lumber at writing,
     liken the efforts
     to a bear's lack of grace
     reaching for a honey comb.
I chance the stings
     as I buzz forth myriad
     thoughts brazenly!

Tanka

Gift

Poised to send forth joy,

Held within each beating heart,

Shared by deed or word,

Stored in infinite supply;

It's free, it's beauty—it's love!

Beauty and Intellect
"Woman as Venus"

Woman as Venus

Sing praise to Venus,
statue of love and beauty,
who is all women.

Seductive to man,
nurturing to child,

sinner and saint,
idealized in prose and paint.

Sing praise to Venus,
though her stone image
flawed woman's role conditioning.

Maternal and beautiful,
no need for mental ability;
missing limbs
limit physical agility.

Sing praise to today's Venus,
no brainless Madonna
encased in marble is she.

Modern woman has unique identity:
mother, mate, beacon to humanity.

Her Majesty

Replete with
    lofty spires,
      turrets and drawbridge.
Sculpted with gold,
    silver and ivory tools
    of dreams.

I reign majestically
    in a castle
    by the sea,
    oblivious of ever-closer
    threatening waves
    you ride.

Drawbridge static,
    no soldiers to defend,
you mount a tidal wave,
    invade my queendom,
    lay siege to my castle,
break its foundation
    and my heart,

wash my sandcastle
    into the sea
    with me.

Woman and Man

A woman belongs to
    no one but herself.
Enslave her,
    a part of her remains free,
    hidden for none to see.

Threaten her young,
    chance clawing;
Betray her,
    suffer wrath—
    escape her path.

Yet she needs, woos, loves man;
    he needs, woos, loves her.
Humbly weak,
    it's sex and love both seek.

As principals in an eternal plan,
    they pursue bliss, mate,
fulfill predestined fate:
heaven's design to procreate …

Abecedarian

A baby is God's opinion that the world should go on.

—Carl Sandburg

A Baby's Cry

A baby's cry

directs everyone

find good, hope,

inspiration, justice,

kindness, love.

Mentor newborn's optimism,

pursuing quick,

revised stereotyping

to undo vicious, wicked,

xenophobia-

yielding zeal!

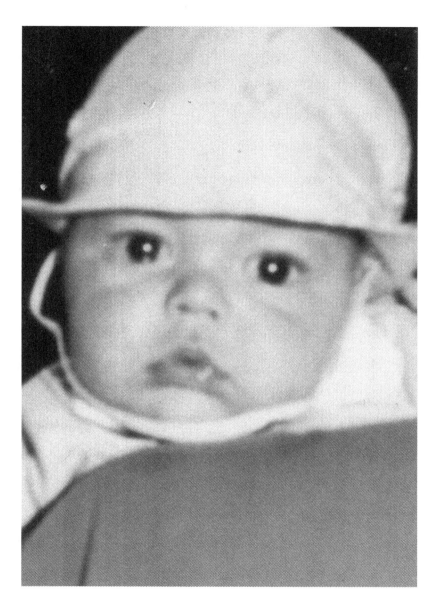

Wondrous New Life:
"A Baby's Cry"

Duo

Wondrous newborn,

how were you fashioned?

Who drew the blueprint

at an enchanted drawing board?

Bid you feed, cry, grow?

Endowed your potential

to think, learn?

Assigned your carrier

to nurture, protect, love you?

Who was the engineer of this

masterful design of perpetuation?

"All rivers flow into the sea,
yet the sea does not overflow."

—Ecclesiastes 1:7

Progeny

I am a river,
emitting my stream
of living creatures
after my kind.

They navigate
in rivulets
    away,
    away,
into rivers of their own,

fashioning life
in their own likenesses.

I am soon
    alone,
    alone,

swallowed by the sea.

Somanka

Tear

From whence comes a tear
　　cascading down
　　　　a visage?

Its sad, mute message,
　　from the windows
　　　　of the soul,
　　　　　　streams from heart
　　　　　　　　to brain to eyes.

In trembled travel,
　　this surging liquid
　　　　floods forth
　　　　　　from pained reservoir.

Shall it be wiped dry,
　　hidden,
　　　　or exposed
　　　　　　for empathy?

Tearful Thoughts
"Tear"

Oh world!, Oh Life!, Oh Time!
On whose last steps I climb.

—Percy Shelley

Sequence

God's child comes forth,
awaits reality
in endless time,
    plays,
    prepares,
    wishes time away,
    courts adulthood.
A time of impatience.

The adult trots with time,
is part of the reality,
    codifies the present,
    contributes to time's pattern,
    makes decisions,
    issues progeny,
    pursues fulfillment,
    succeeds,
    fails.
A time of involvement.

The senior rushes to keep
pace with time,
    questions final reality,
    strives to achieve,
    reflects,
    laments the past,
    reaches for longevity,
    relaxes,
    slows,
    seeks immortality.
A time to return to God.

Wondrous Death

The pearly gates open.
A smiling angel releases me
from my earthly body,

grants me winged mobility—
enchanted freedom, high in the heavens.

I leap from cloud to cloud,
attaching to mosaic forms;

I run the arch of the
rainbow's alternating colors;

I fly with birds,
circling the sky;

I join the downward trip
of life-giving sunbeams;

I dance with the angels
as they bless God's nests
of the unborn;

I enter stars that shine
for eternity;

I am free of body—
to joyfully revel in the mysteries
of nature's phenomena.

Hell Waiting

Have you ever wondered what
your personal perdition might be?
If my sins are unforgiven,
I know there's one waiting for me.

I see a woman driving
a loaded tractor-trailer.
She cannot escape;
the truck is her jailer.

There is a steep hill
she's ascending,
The route unfamiliar, unpaved,
bumpy, unending.

Straining to survey the road,
view obscured by seat's height,
she leans forward, moves from left to right,
follows dictates of traffic lights.

She must turn many corners,
truck's rear in pursuit,
causing drivers concern
as she blocks their planned route.

The scenario is my
custom-made hell,
fashioned by Beelzebub—
he knows me very well.

I'm a woman driver.
I've been damned to hell!

Joyous Paint

Colors borrowed
from rainbow, sea, and sky
shine, gladden,
deceive happily,
cover the new,
encourage artistry.

Woman's painted face
simulates blushing youth:
rosy cheeks,
bright red lips—
temporary beauty
brings joy in vanity.

Clown's painted face,
sad, drooping mouth,
falling tears,
jocular antics,
state clown's aim:
laugh at self-deception,
hide the sad, be glad,
mask reality.

Brush me with paint:
I am a clown!

Versatile Dancing

Activating beauty,

circuitous dancing

envelops fleeting gladness.

Healthful, invigorating,

joyful, kinetic,

lithe mobility

now offers personal,

quiet reaction;

sometimes tantalizing,

undulating variation

wields X-rated,

youthful zigzagging.

Static Lovers
"Woeful Adolescence"

Keats, in his poem "Ode on a Grecian Urn," writes of the futile chase of the static lovers on the urn, who remain young and forever fair without the realism of passing time.

Woeful Adolescence

Two children—caught in
magnificent magnetism,
bewildered by emotion—
flounder with immaturity,
ignore passing time.

Sated with
brush of lips,
touch of hand,
they function chastely
with idealistic modesty,
painful inhibition,
mute voices.

Sadly separated by fate,
memory of youth and beauty
eternal,
unchanged by
ravages of time,
objective check
with reality.

(continues on next page)

Young love's fruition is
forever suspended,
like the futile
chase of Keats's figures
embossed on the Grecian urn,

the unattainable,
doomed
to be coveted
forever ...

Empty

A now-familiar scene of impending doom:
The iron bed, table, basin, chair of the hospital room.

The pretty, frail patient spoke: "The pain won't go away."
"Until it does, mother, I'll stay."

My husband, with rational approach, argued against it.
"It might be months she'll be this way.
Can you stay here night and day?"

I left with heavy heart
and planned for an early-morning start.

Morning came.
A shock wave engulfed my being!
I stared in disbelief at what I was seeing!

Surely she's on another floor or in a different room!
But it had come: doom!
The bed was stripped and empty!

- - - - - - - - - - - - -

She filled the dark, empty hole of the gravesite,
never again to see the light.

We empty her home of its spoils,
pride of her life's toils.

(continues on next page)

We walk through the empty rooms,
echoing footsteps signifying gloom.

Hear me! This is the promise I made:
"I shall not leave until the pain will fade."

Empty bed! Empty promise! Heart filled with guilt
in my forever!

Helpless

It's a Svengali affair:
He says, "Come," and I am there,
walking into it—each time,
an unknown dimension of fear.

Playing into his hands,
magnetically drawn to the web he spins—
this man who gives me dental care
has me hanging helpless.
Reticent automaton.

Encumbrance in my mouth
keeps me from talking.
He chats of world events,
speaks of family,
tries to distract me.
Amiable man.

On escorting me to the door,
he, smiling, reports:
"Just one more visit
on the first root canal;
only two more to go."
Monstrous man!

As I'm bolting for the door,
I think,
I've heard of painless dentistry—
why hasn't he?
I vow to ask him next time;
right now I'm out of here.
Happy escapee!

Sad Hide and Seek

Like the tides that ebb and flow
refuse to recede and culminate,
she is exiled into oblivion,
pays visits to reality,
returns to her prison.

What internal battle conquered her,
so loquacious, now mute,
so sparkling, now dull?
How can I infuse life into this shell?
I look into her eyes,
now vacant and unknowing.

Can I ignite the spark of life,
perhaps with sibling memories?
She has left us with no connecting doorway.
I find myself banging on the non-existent
doorway, demanding entrance!

Limited Vision
"Limiting Horizons"

A horizon is nothing save the
limit of our sight.

—R. W. Raymond

Limiting Horizons

Phantom junctions rendezvous

with land, sea, and sky,

as horizons to our eye

confine, deceive, imprison,

subject to mocking, deserved derision.

The brave have challenged

terminal lines,

searchlighted infinite avenues,

refused to be confined.

Do I seek to ignite the nuclei

of my meager conceptions,

challenge my blind,

limiting perceptions?

To whom do I offer timid excuse?

A New Day

Yesterday's sadness is in the past;

today's heart wakens to heavy pain,

yet a stream of light escapes

through the closed shutter.

One flick of the cord

brings sunshine

and new horizons to view.

Theater

Don the actor's mask;
abandon the mundane.

Suspend your disbeliefs;
believe in miracles.

Share a lover's kiss;
feel the passion.

Scream with inner fear;
beseech the villain's mercy.

Laugh uproariously;
shed decorum.

Support the hero's cause;
applaud his victory.

Move with dancing feet;
borrow imagined flight.

Sing with the soprano;
rise to her crescendos.

Be inspired; mask reality;
pursue wonder.

Dramatize, suffer, enjoy, delight;
participate in the magic of theater.

Inconsistent Time
"Time with You"

Time with You

The clock is a time-honored,
mechanical metronome;
punctuating before, soon, now, after;
never deviating its regulated tick;
incapable of changing from
slow to quick.

Then why sadly lament,
"Time drags—why is it so slow?"
or joyfully proclaim,
"Time flew so fast!
Where did it go?"

It's we, not time
who are capricious.
Awaiting you,
time drags sadly by.
With you, time is
wondrously winged to fly.

So love, won't you stay
to seek our destiny?
Share my before, soon, now, after?
Fly time away happily
with me?

Ageless Elvis

I saw him!
I went ballistic!
He was on stage!
Did he hear my shrill scream
join others?
"I love you, Elvis!"
Elvis adulation was
all the rage.

He wore a red bandana.
It was a great show!
He sang for me.
He played for me.
The bond between us
was all aglow!

Years have passed.
He still has appeal,
though he'd be pushing sixty-five;
ghost of the ideal.

Hair thinning,
stomach rounded,
youth finished,
the toxic glow still glimmers,
though it should be diminished.

The early deaths of Elvis
and Marilyn, too, were tragic,
but their young images are alive
through fond memory and
technology's magic.

- - - -

I love you, Elvis!

Her Adam

He told her she was the
    apple of his eye.
She treasured this avowal
    of love on which to rely.

Wasn't the tantalizing apple
    the historic instrument
    of man's fate?

Wasn't Eve's bond with Adam
    the apple's primal role,
destined to embrace
    the continuity of the
human race?

But had she truly been the
    apple of his eye,
would he have chewed her up,
    spit out the seed?

Was he punished—blinded by
    his heinous deed?

    Applesauce!

Social Issues

"If we do not learn to live together as brothers, then we shall die as fools."

—Dr. Martin Luther King, Jr.

9-1-1

If we all looked and functioned the same,
how
dull.

Differences

It must have been in heaven
that the Supreme Artist
fashioned flowers in varied hues—
reds, yellows, oranges, blues—
each with unique design,
creating a multicolored bouquet
of grace, perfume, and beauty.

It had to be in heaven
that the Supreme Artist
fashioned humans in varied hues—
white, brown, tan on review,
each with unique potential,
creating a multicultural bouquet
of hope, global progress, and beauty.

Twin Towers
"The Terror"

The Terror

The Terror knows no border,
has no limited geographics,
is not fenced in.
There is no end to the tragic din.

Its genocide blisters, burgeons,
bursts forth,
masked in the name of divine instruction,
armed with promised reward, in afterlife,
for self-destruction.

With wounded cry and prayer,
we wonder what the consequences will be,
await resolute unity of nations
to terminate the Terror tragedy.

September 11, 2001: Two Minutes Left

Fear darts in and out of his eyes,
focuses on vague horizons;

unleashing its force to transfer
to the unknown,
yet to be confronted;

grasps the shadowy
chain of terror,

transmitting it furtively
to unheeding space,
spinning a dust-filled shroud....

Then peace banishes fear,
lifting the soul
to a heavenly sphere.

I will maintain my covenant with you [Noah and his sons], never again shall all flesh be cut off by the waters of a flood, and never again shall there be a flood to destroy the earth.

—Genesis 9:7

Water, Agent of Life; Water, Agent of Death

Contemplation on Tsunami

I am water, agent of life.

I am water, the survival elixir for humans
and all flora and fauna, awaiting release in
ethereal cloud formation.

I drop to thirsty earth to bid seed grant
life to edible plants, beautiful foliage, with
the sun's grace.

I appear as the rain and snowflakes in unique design.

I create the phenomena of babbling brooks, placid
lakes, flowing falls and rivers, undulating oceans.

I am water, agent of death.

I manipulate undulating oceans, vent fury and
destruction with thunder storms, earthquakes, and flood.

I functioned as God's instrument of death by flood
and tsunami, and thus communicated warning to man.
(continues on next page)

In His design, my destruction was restricted by His covenant with Noah and his sons, decreeing: "The water shall never again become a flood to destroy all flesh that is on earth."

I, water, was commanded to flood by tsunami as warning to man to halt genocide, war, and inhumanities.

If man continues his errant ways, the wrath of God shall be incurred, and man will be annihilated in a fashion of
      His choice.
      I, water, beseech man to take heed.
      I am water, agent of life and death.

The "New" New Orleans

Host to tourists and conventions,
    New Orleans was a city of joy.
Hotels loomed high to house visitors.
Cobblestone streets, lined with
        restaurants and cavorting horses
            and buggies,
        boasted buildings with wrought-
        iron window grilles.
There was no clue the happy scene
    was destined to be stilled!

Then Hurricane Katrina's
    devastation came.
New Orleans was now a city of
    turmoil and pain:
        Families fled, sought to relocate.
A count of the dead proved difficult
    to calculate.

New Orleans citizens seek heavenly
    guidance to rebuild,
        fight psychological aftermath,
        follow an optimistic, successful path
        for the birth of a

    "New" New Orleans.

A memorial to Nixzmary and Quachon Browne, victims of fatal child abuse.

The Neophyte

I'm coiled
in sweet, temperate darkness,
stretching with anatomical growth
    in a womb,
subject to my ejector's condition.

I arrive a guiltless neophyte,
released to the positives and negatives
    of an alien world.

I'm the lucky child,
subject to sweet sound and touch,
perhaps destined to make this a
better world.

I'm the unlucky child,
subject to dysfunctional family.
Will I be neglected, starved,
    abused, maimed, killed?
Surviving, will I alone buffer
    my condition,
or adopt the undesirable:
withdrawal, drugs, crime?

Perhaps I'm destined to make
    this a better world.
Who will respond to the stifled
    cries of the hapless child?
School, social agency? You, I?

On May 31, 2002, a memorial was held at the Trade Center Memorial Site, titled "A Silent Goodbye."

Defying the Silence of "The Silent Goodbye":

Challenge to Closure

Hushed audience awaits the bells' tolls:
    Four sets of rings signal forward
    a flagged, empty stretcher
    filled with beloved heroes'
    invisible souls.

Silence prevails
in newly voided airspace,
permeated with love, grief,
and thanks for terror heroes of
every color, creed, and race.

Quiet prayer, reverent
salute, seek solace
in closure pursuit.

Then sound pierces silence,
rhythmic drums beat,
doleful bagpipes whine,
a child cries;
they negate, defy defeat.

(continues on next page)

Next, penetrating taps,
and in procession
stretcher, Column I
marchers, all loudly
proclaim, "America
shall ever be crowned,
from sea to shining sea."

Spontaneous applause erupts,
challenges tragic toll,
declares invincible defiance
to the determined rat-a-tat
of the drums' roll.
Rat-a-tat, rat-a-tat, rat-a-tat ...

Heroic Death
"Korean Memorial"

Korean Memorial

No tender blanket of grass,
no list of names on plaques of stone,
but towering figures of the military,
impressive to our gaze.

Marching forward,
engulfed in the business of war.

Multifaceted stone background of
varied colors,
perhaps imaging
multicultural endeavor:
Marching forward.

Dignity and determination
etched in furrowed brows,
endeavoring to mend
a fractured world
seeking freedom's promise.
Marching forward.

Stumbling in venues
of self-sacrifice,
saving others,
rage and blood prefacing
death and doom.
Marching forward.

Emerging victorious
in death,
fostering our nation's
eternal life.
Marching forward!

The Sad Tour

The entrance sign to the memorial site
    read: Auschwitz;
its arched wrought-iron motto:
Arbeit macht frei—"Work makes one free."
So narrow an entrance, no more than six feet—
the portal to hell
for millions.

Herded from trains, they staggered forward, clutching meager
    possessions,
to survey a high, electrified barbed wire fence.

With what bewildered appraisal
did they view
three-tiered brick bunks
crowded into small rooms?

What did they believe
about the undressing and shaving of heads
as they were prepared for "showers"?

Did they become aware
of the gas chambers
with their first gasps?
Did they call out to God,
scream the names of loved ones?

Could tourists detect a
residual odor
of bodies burned
in the large crematoria?

Were there echoes
of loud protests
by slave workers
as identification numbers were seared
into the soft flesh of their arms?

Was there a haunting sound
of inmates' shovels
as mass graves were dug
for some of the dead?

How many of the rebellious
did the watchtower machine gun kill?

What was the count of the shabby suitcases,
men's, women's, and children's shoes
displayed in showcases,
each representing a lost soul?

Is it possible
that the deceased
heard six tourists
recite the Hebrew mourners' prayer
for them and
martyred relatives
at the tour's end?

What lesson was learned
from the victims' sacrifice?
How long is "never again"?

The sleeping bunks

Photographed by
Sol Rubin

Auschwitz

"The Sad Tour"

A plea in six languages

Photographed by
Sol Rubin

Auschwitz

"The Sad Tour"

Hidden Graves
"Gravestones"

Carl Sandburg's "Grass" contends that "grass works" to cover gravesites of heroes, eventually converting cemetery land to commercial use. "I am grass. Let me work."

Gravestones

(With apology to religious conviction)

Grass overgrows the grave sites,
obscuring stones' etchings,
decreeing anonymity.

Deathstones hidden,
footsteps tread foliage
and desecrate the sacred sites unknowingly.

Burdened by soil atop them
lie remains of
earthly flesh and blood,
now dormant, full of death,
destined to dust.

Once mourned with ripples of tears,
issue now long gone,
none to seek the grass be cut;
none to rue what once was man.

What is the measure of mourning time?
Is land for the use of the living?
Do the disassembled dead care?

Skeletons sleep.

Lower East Side Tenement Museum

Tiny rooms,
balanced each
atop another;
six-story brick stage
for Jewish, Italian, Irish
immigrants
trudging wooden steps,
mounting skyward
their gateway to America.

Hearts smoldering in
burning hope,
clutching immigrant dreams:
freedom; opportunity;
golden, glittering streets—
but finding muddy reality:
slop pails, crowding, hunger,
illness, sweatshops.

Undaunted new
fusion of humanity
searched identity,
held hands,
kept faith,
raised families,
struggled, cried,
learned, sang,
reveled in the will
to succeed,

then took flight!
Burgeoning citizens
on the morrow of a new world,
contributing multicultural
talents to its image,
touching its shape.

Boys Must Be Boys

It's difficult to be a boy growing up, they say,
yet boys would not have it the other way.

Boys, you must be brave in all you do;
pretty girls expect you to.

Do not show fear—
surely never when girls are near.

        Learn to sweet-talk girls, promise bliss.
Girls act coy, yet solicit this.

Courtesy rules are all set up for show:
        "Ladies first" is one to know.

Boys must never, ever cry:
be manly; stay dry-eyed.

        Sports involvement is a must;
get into sports or be a bust.

Since girls are the weaker sex,
boys, be strong; bulging muscles shout:
"Pretty girls, check me out!"

Yet act as if there's much you know—
not just brawn, but brains must show.

It's difficult to be a boy growing up, they say,
yet boys would not have it the other way.

Shuttle Columbia

The awaited triumphant return to Earth of
shuttle *Columbia*, bringing space mission data,
tragically failed!
On its return trip from orbit, the spaceship *Columbia*—
and its seven astronauts—splintered into space.

How can we rationalize this horrific event?
Perhaps we are meant to
channel our energies
under the deceased astronauts'
heavenly aegis.

Is it possible we are destined to reverently seek
their divine guidance as ethereal mentors,
to bless and direct efforts
as we seek to escalate exploration?

The seven astronauts have honored
their pledge to risk their lives
to further mankind's progress.
We pledge to honor them forever!

Abecedarian

Merriam-Webster's Dictionary's definition of omnipotent: *"All powerful, having unlimited authority."*

Brainless Omnipotent Bells

Authoritative bells

control, delineate events;

force, guide,

halt, initiate, judge,

keep limits,

measure.

Naggingly omnipotent.

People quickly respond.

Stimulated to unequivocally verify

with X-ray,

yields zilch.

I Chose, I Fear, I Must

I chose
    the thin gold band
        encircling my finger
            that now imprisons me.

I fear
    hearing his key in the door,
        his mood,
            being beaten,
                moving out with no place to go,
                some day being killed,
                    leaving my babies alone.

I must
    not tell anyone,
        hide my bruises,
            convince the children he loves us,
            believe he's really sorry
            and will change.

- - - - - - - - - - - - -

I must get dinner ready now.

Candidates' Debate

Let's debate.
Voters are listening to our prepared programs
replete with litanies of words,
responding to the challenge of promises
already heard.

Let's be polite,
contest and protest,
display sharp wit but not incite,
don masks of vulnerable friendliness
as we fight.

Let's evade.
We're not ready to call
a spade a spade.
Though we're down to the finish line,
polished yet convoluted oratory
will shine.

Let's be fair and square tonight,
or even legally triangular or octangular—
any which way to succeed
will be the crowned winner's delight.

The Public and the Not-So-Merry Political Scene

Donning a questionable mask of selflessness
and righteous devotion,
embellished with oratory eloquence
and emotion,
each politician spouts obtuse promises
that astonish.
Woe to opponents, challengers admonish.

We attend political-meeting venues,
listen to campaign menus,
then watchdog political replay,
study platforms, funding sources,
quotes, past record, morals, personalities.
They know we critique continually!

We voters are wooed, choices will be made.
After election, our powers fade.

Nature:
Flora & Fauna

The Gates

Nature's beauty is inherently drama.
The Gates display proved to be a long-
    awaited nature and social diorama.
Thousands came from near and far:
    some judged it genius; some bizarre.

The Gates set a stage for visitors to
    commune with nature—
twenty-two miles it ran—
    and also to commune with fellow man.

On the peripatetic route, strangers
    happily greeted strangers,
    clasped hands, exchanged backgrounds,
    benevolent words, and smiles
    as they walked portions of the
    serpentine-winding miles.

Treading the unknown,
    if you will, perhaps to peer ahead,
    seeking preview to the biblical,
    culminating "Gates of Heaven,"
    as in biblical lore it is said.

Quick Succession

Spring rushes summer,
    and the promise of fall
    is the early overcast in summer.
    Autumn quickly calls forth winter.

How soon fall bloom diminishes
    to decay and barrenness,
    signaling winter death.

Then heaven decrees the miracle
    of withholding
    shattering frost,
    to nurture withered flora
    with the promise of spring,
and impatient seasonal continuity.

Windblown
"Autumn Leaves"

Somanka

Autumn Leaves

Autumn winds blow;
umbilical stems loosen.
Once green, moist, and supple,
now dry, curled, yellowed
leaves fly—victims
of wind's caprices.

Impelled to motion,
float solo at varied speed,
move in groups, form piles;
lifting, shifting, breaking, doomed
wild performers—Dance of Death.

Nature's Mood Music

Without voice but
with bold sound,
like a clarion call
of Joshua's trumpet
heralding battle,
it rages and ravages,
howling and gusting.

At times, it whistles
arrival,
like a train announcing
destination.

It evokes sweet song,
interludes of melody
amid swaying leaves
and stalks of green.

Silently it pushes,
directs some objects take
quiet flight,
others to move noisily
with rhythmic beat.

Vocal though mute,
present yet unseen,
making known to the moon
its capricious moods
caged therein for release.

Snow's Cascade

Snow cascades
in frozen silence,
blankets in pristine white;
bids pause in time,
reflection on beauty,
on primal innocence;

begs rejection
of worldly corruption;
covers tides of bigotry,
seas of ravage,
oceans of genocide;

speaks its mute message,
soon melted—
desecrated—by
dark gargoyles
of reality.

Ethereal snow
implores we emulate
its purity,
evidence of godliness …

Cinquain

Untitled

Ice storm

lends trees mock bloom;

bare, skeletal branches

are dressed in iridescent ice,

gleaming.

Untitled

Budding

pledge of new growth

Goddess Flora assists,

unfolds burgeoning petal joy

preview.

A Deciduous Winter Tree's Love Ode to the Sun

The Angel of Death
spread his wings over me.

I was waxed deadly
in autumn denouement
and winter shroud.

Gray and skeletal,
smote by the sword
of the soil's frigidity,
no dew anointed me.

Then your warm kiss
pierced the frigid soil,
Infused life into my being,
climbed my skeletal arms,

aroused a burgeoning
umbrella of green,
arched thereto a plethora
of scented blossoms
magically culminating
in a harvest of fruition.

I lift my limbs ever skyward
in homage, embraced
by the secret of the sun.

Spring

What heralds spring?
Are chirping birds assigned
to alert the sun,
to warm the ground,
to make soil fertile,
to break seed covers,
to absorb the rain,
to summon bees,
to chauffeur pollen,
to pistillate seed,
to bring us floral beauty,
to intoxicate?

I am drunk with spring!

Nature's Attractions
"Renewal: Tree and Woman"

Renewal:
Tree And Woman

The mulberry tree's beauty
seductive to birds,
with plethora of ripe berries;
woman's beauty seductive to man,
with breast and supple body.

The tree proudly presents
repetitive summers' crescendos
with falling and growing seed.

The woman stands proudly
for her summers of crescendos
ejecting and nurturing seed.

The tree repeats fertility
with longevity,
seasonally awakening
to warmth and youth.

Seasons finite,
woman goes to final slumber
in dark oblivion.
Her élan vitale perpetuates
in generations of seed.

There is beauty
and underlying pattern in nature.

Deceitful Flower
"Dandelion"

Dandelion

Dandelion—
yellow circlet of petals,
stem of green,
pretty little wild flower—
you spoil the garden scene.

Your presence spreads.
Through the grass you sway,
roots eclipsing innocent blades
as night the day.

You deceive
and change to angelic fuzz,
ready to sail off
when the wind will blow,
dropping destructive seed
as you go.

Your grace is beguiling;
children blow you apart
with delight.
In wonder, they watch your flight.

True, you're pretty and even fun,
but we see the damage you've done.

It must be said:
"You kill grass.
You're not nice!"

"Moonlight"

The moon fell into the lake one summer night.

It shone brightly—conversely,

its light eclipsing darkness.

It made not a splash

but sat in stillness,

exuding beauty.

I tried to lift it out

to embrace it,

but it serenely smiled

and to my touch

left in fleeting evanescence.

Static Runner
"Carousel"

Carousel

Bejeweled, mirrored, flowered pony,
mounted on a post
that carries you up and down
on a continuously revolving stage;
head coned in pastel color,
children sitting in matching saddles
while the carousel's calliope plays.

Bringing smiles,
do you smile too
gifted quadruped runner,
poised for motion,
yet static;
playing benevolent host
to kicks on your painted body,
little fingers exploring your eyes,
pulling your tail?

Are you longing for magical endowment,
to trot away to freedom,
finding fields of grass on which to roam,
tasting greenness,
risking a broken spirit
to be recaptured,
tamed,
again harnessed, bridled, captive
instrument of man's work and pleasure?
(continues on next page)

Stay safely mounted,
smiling with the children,
keeping pace with the music,
bejeweled, mirrored, flowered pony,
while the carousel's calliope plays.

Who's Birdbrained?

Man assigns the vernacular term
    "birdbrained" to someone not bright.
        My fine, non-feathered friend,
            that assumption is not right.

We birds are artfully hued
    and feathered to fly.
        You invent fallible machines
        to simulate our gift
            of circling the sky.

Our many species sing
    in heaven-sent voice.
        You imperfectly imitate
        our fine song choice.

Encased in fragile body, we survive:
    nest, rear young, forage for food,
        communicate, migrate,
            happily stay alive.

Truly, birds are spectacular.
    Please delete the term
        "birdbrained" from
            your vernacular.

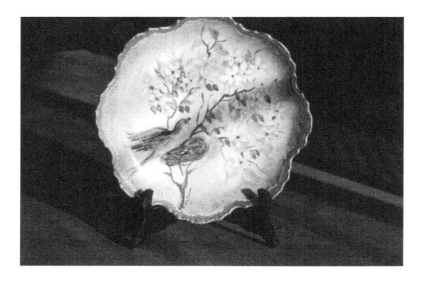

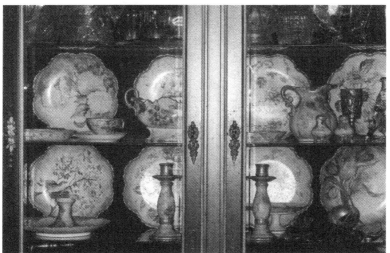

Feathered Cleverness among Flowers
"Who's Birdbrained?"

About the Author

Bea's poetry has appeared in numerous publications, including anthologies. She is a frequent featured presenter at New York City poetry venues. Bea's background includes being a teacher, a guidance counselor, and an adjunct assistant professor at Kingsborough Community College (where a text she authored was utilized). She is a member of the Phi Beta Kappa and Kappa Delta Pi honor societies, and is involved in community activities.

978-0-595-42656-0
0-595-42656-5

www.ingramcontent.com/pod-product-compliance
Lightning Source LLC
Chambersburg PA
CBHW051254050326
40689CB00007B/1193